THE FACTS ON FALSE VIEWS OF JESUS

John Ankerberg & John Weldon

HARVEST HOUSE PUBLISHERS
Eugene, Oregon 97402

Unless otherwise indicated, Scripture verses are taken from the New International Version®, Copyright © 1973, 1978, 1984 by the International Bible Society. Used by permission of Zondervan Publishing House. The "NIV" and "New International Version" trademarks are registered in the United States Patent and Trademark Office by the International Bible Society.

Other books by
John Ankerberg & John Weldon

The Facts on Abortion	The Facts on Near-Death Experiences
The Facts on Angels	The Facts on the New Age Movement
The Facts on Astrology	The Facts on the Occult
The Facts on Creation vs. Evolution	The Facts on Psychic Readings
The Facts on the Faith Movement	The Facts on Rock Music
The Facts on False Teaching in the Church	The Facts on Roman Catholicism
The Facts on Halloween	The Facts on Self Esteem, Psychology, and the Recovery Movement
The Facts on Hinduism	The Facts on Spirit Guides
The Facts on Holistic Health and the New Medicine	The Facts on UFO's and Other Supernatural Phenomena
The Facts on Homosexuality	Knowing the Truth About Jesus the Messiah
The Facts on Islam	Knowing the Truth About the Resurrection
The Facts on the Jehovah's Witnesses	Knowing the Truth About Salvation
The Facts on the King James Only Debate	Knowing the Truth About the Trinity
The Facts on Life After Death	
The Facts on the Masonic Lodge	
The Facts on the Mind Sciences	
The Facts on the Mormon Church	

THE FACTS ON FALSE VIEWS OF JESUS
Copyright © 1997 by The John Ankerberg Show
Published by Harvest House Publishers
Eugene, Oregon 97402

ISBN 1-56507-692-3

All rights reserved. No portion of this book may be used in any form without the written permission of the Publishers.

Printed in the United States of America.

97 98 99 00 01 02 03 04 / LP / 10 9 8 7 6 5 4 3 2 1

Contents

The Gathering Storm in the Church

Section I
The Jesus Seminar

1. How do liberal theologians see Jesus? 6
2. What is the Jesus Seminar? 8
3. What did the Jesus Seminar conclude about Jesus and His teachings? 9
4. Why should liberal theologians be trusted? 12
5. What are liberal theologians responsible for? .. 16
6. What are the major problems with the Jesus Seminar? 17
7. What is the enigmatic "Q"? Where is it? 23
8. What should be rejected—the New Testament or the liberal critics? 26

Section II
Higher Criticism, the Bible, and the Church

9. Is higher critical methodology necessarily opposed to God and His Word? 31
10. Are the benefits to the church worth the risk? . 34

Recommended Reading 41

Notes.................................. 43

The Gathering Storm in the Church

In modern times, many enlightened types have become skeptical, and we look down on the uneducated types who believe. It's sort of a pity that all most know about Jesus is from the creeds which we can't believe.[1]

> —James Robinson,
> of the Jesus Seminar and
> the International Q
> Project

As for the person who hears my words but does not keep them, I do not judge him. For I did not come to judge the world, but to save it. There is a judge for the one who rejects me and does not accept my words; that very word which I spoke will condemn him at the last day. For I did not speak of my own accord, but the Father who sent me commanded me what to say and how to say it. I know that his command leads to eternal life. So whatever I say is just what the Father has told me to say (John 12:47-50).

In April 1996 something unique happened in the history of publishing. In their April 8, 1996 issues, three major news magazines carried cover stories on Jesus Christ.[2] Even two thousand years after He died, Jesus continues to impact the secular world more than any other person in history. Certainly the world seems to be fascinated by Him and, naturally, so are His followers.

However, if recent poll results are valid, many people—including, ironically, Christians—are more confused about Jesus and biblical authority than ever before. At the Evangelical Ministries to the New Religions National Conference on September 12, 1996, Dr. John Ankerberg, in his lecture entitled "Characteristics of the People and False Religion of the Last Days," stated:

> According to the recent polls of George Gallup, George Barna, and James D. Hunter, 35% of America's Evangelical seminarians deny that faith in Christ is absolutely necessary. What's even more alarming is that 35% of the entire adult evangelical population agrees with the statement: "God will save all good people when they die, regardless of whether they've trusted in Christ."
> ... *Pulpit Helps* revealed that a survey of 7,441 Protestant pastors [51% Methodist; 35% Presbyterian;

33% Baptist; 30% Episcopalian] did not believe in the physical resurrection of Jesus.

Another alarming statistic is that 77% of America's evangelicals believe that human beings are basically good by nature, whereas, the Scripture says man was created good but fell and now has a sinful nature. Instead of evangelical preaching that man is utterly condemned and helpless as a result of his sin and can do nothing to save himself, recent surveys have shown that 87% of American evangelicals hold to the idea that "God helps those who help themselves."

Consider other polls by the George Barna organization. These are even more disconcerting. In one 1991 poll, "53% of those claiming to be Bible-believing conservative Christians said there is no such thing as absolute truth." In another poll, 43% of born-again Christians agreed that "it does not matter what religious faith you follow because all faiths teach similar lessons about life." According to *Newsweek*, April 8, 1996, "A survey conducted last month by the Barna Research Group, a conservative Christian organization in California, finds that 30% of 'born-again' Christians do not believe that 'Jesus came back to physical life after he was crucified.'"[3]

Obviously something is wrong since these beliefs are not biblical. Either these results are incorrect or people are claiming they are genuine Christians when they are not. Another possibility is that many people in the church have bought a bill of goods. How did Christians ever get such terrible misinformation in the first place?

Given the declining moral and intellectual trend in our culture in the last generation and its influence in the church, these results are not entirely unexpected. But in all the places one may look to explain such results, an often overlooked area is liberal theology and its "higher critical" approach to the Bible. This critical approach is widely endorsed by mainstream theologians and denominations, many critics of the Bible, and cults like Mormonism, and world religions such as Islam, which have a vested interest in seeking to discredit biblical Christianity.[4] Strangely, these destructive methods are increasingly being used even by some evangelical scholars.

Because of our convictions as to the seriousness of this issue, a critique of liberal theology is important—

even vital. However, it should not be forgotten that the final disproof of theological liberalism is not just in its terminally flawed assumptions and methods, but in the positive evidence for the historic reliability of the New Testament picture of Christ and the Bible as a whole. Although we touch the evidence supporting the Bible, we have also prepared a companion volume, *Knowing the Truth About the Reliability of the Bible*, that provides a more in-depth look at the facts confirming the accuracy of God's Word.

SECTION I

The Jesus Seminar

1. *How do liberal theologians see Jesus?*

There is no denying the fact that once trust in the Bible as an authoritative source is undermined, its teachings will either be doubted or, considered irrelevant. Yet we don't think that most Christians, especially the average American, have any idea of the great weight of blame that can be laid at the feet of "liberal theology" and higher criticism for destroying America's faith in the Bible—or the terrible consequences socially, morally, and spiritually that must logically flow from it.

To illustrate the "liberal approach" to the Bible we will cite the findings of the Jesus Seminar (JS), an endeavor of 74 liberal scholars to determine what Jesus "really" said, as well as the all too common view of Scripture seen in popular news magazines.

Almost every year, especially at Easter and Christmas, news magazines comment about all the books written by liberal theologians in the search for the "historical Jesus," the alleged enigmatic "real" Jesus of history, as opposed to the "Christ of faith" that is found in the Bible and who Christians believe in. In recent years, dozens of books have been written by liberal and non-evangelical theologians rejecting or attacking the very foundation of the Christian faith: the biblical Jesus Christ. Among these books are John Dominic Crossan's *Jesus: A Revolutionary Biography; The Historical Jesus: The Life of a Mediterranean Jewish Peasant* and *Who Killed Jesus?*; Burton Mack's *Who Wrote the New Testament: The Making of the Christian Myth*, *A Myth of Innocence: Mark and Christian Origins*, and *The Lost Gospel: The Book of Q and Christian Origins*; Robert

Funk's *Honest to Jesus*; and the book published by the Jesus Seminar, *The Five Gospels: The Search for the Authentic Words of Jesus.*[5]

In liberal theology books, we find Jesus is portrayed in a diverse manner—as a Jewish holy man, an occult magician and mystic, a personification of a psychedelic mushroom cult, a homosexual, a twice-married divorcé with three kids, a wicked priest, a social cynic, a political revolutionary, and just about any other view one might wish to take. According to Gregory Boyd, theology professor at Bethel College in St. Paul, Minnesota and author of *Cynic, Sage or Son of God?* "Perhaps the most intriguing part of this modern quest [for the historical Jesus] is how the interests and personalities of scholars intersect with their work. The 'control-beliefs of a scholar . . . determine what kind of Jesus he or she is looking for by defining what kind of Jesus is and is not possible.' That is why examining the lives of leaders in the historical-Jesus movement is a key to understanding their findings."[6] In other words, these scholars are more concerned with writing about a Jesus they are personally comfortable with rather than accepting the Jesus we find in the four Gospels.

Consider that many writings of liberal theologians have received wide publicity, not only from magazines such as *Time* and *Newsweek*, but TV specials also. No wonder they're having such an impact! As an article in *Time* magazine points out, "There's an enormous appetite among ordinary churchgoers [who] are very puzzled about what's going on."[7]

But puzzled isn't quite the appropriate word. We think that Christians who are not grounded in theology and apologetics and aren't aware of the problems of historical criticism and the "search for the historical Jesus" are having their faith damaged, often greatly, by exposure to these materials. It's a much more serious issue than merely being puzzled. The poll results cited previously are proof enough.

Luke Timothy Johnson, a Roman Catholic scholar who is critical of the Jesus Seminar, comments quite correctly that "people have no idea how fraudulent people who claim to be scholars can be."[8] Further, citing another problem, "Americans generally have an abysmal level of knowledge of the Bible. In this world of mass ignorance, to have headlines proclaim that this or that fact about [Jesus] has been declared untrue by supposedly scientific inquiry has the effect of gospel. There is no basis on which most people can counter these authoritative-sounding statements." (See note 9.)

2. What is the Jesus Seminar?

The Jesus Seminar (JS) aptly illustrates the subtly deceptive reasoning of liberal critical biblical scholarship in general. In 1993, the conclusions by the JS were published in a large, detailed text titled *The Five Gospels: The Search for the Authentic Words of Jesus*.

> The scholars have taken the keys of knowledge and hidden them (Thomas 39:1,* cited in *The Five Gospels*, p. x.)

According to the *Los Angeles Times* (November 25, 1978), when the Jesus Seminar was first loosely organized it had only several members and hoped to enlist 12 to 15 biblical authorities to vote on every word of Jesus to decide which were the most authentic and which were "put into his mouth" by early church tradition. Project organizer Robert W. Funk, a former president of the Society of Biblical Literature, said the purpose of the seminar was to determine what Jesus *really* said.

Harvard Divinity School's George MacRae, one of the first members of the group, said that the real question the scholars would be asking was: "What can we say Jesus said after 60 years of form criticism, of analyzing individual miracle stories and sayings?"

The *Los Angeles Times* pointed out that some evangelical scholars would be added to the Seminar (back then it was simply a committee), "but only those who use modern critical methods," according to MacRae. Eight years later, the impact of the JS was beginning to be felt.

An article by John Dart in *Los Angeles Times*, quoting Van Harvey (chairman of Stanford University's Religious Studies department), pointed out, "So far as the biblical historian is concerned, there is scarcely a popularly held traditional belief about Jesus that is not regarded with considerable skepticism."[10] Harvey implied that the layman, i.e. the average Christian, really isn't qualified to understand the Bible or assess

---
* Considered a fifth Gospel by the JS, the "Gospel of Thomas" is fraudulent and gnostic.

its various claims. "The Stanford professor said that New Testament scholarship has become so specialized and requires so much preparation that many scholars feel 'the lay person has simply been disqualified from having any right to a judgment regarding the truth or falsity of certain historical claims.'"[11]

That's like saying the average American has been *disqualified* from and has *no right* to judge the truth of certain specialized political claims!

Further, John Dart reported, "The lay person unacquainted with New Testament research is no more in a position to have an informed judgment on the historical reliability of gospel accounts than a non-specialist would about 'the Seventh Letter of Plato, the relationship of Montezuma to Cortez' or other historical matters."

So, most Christians really aren't qualified to say anything about the words of Jesus. Only the liberal scholars are so qualified. "Unfortunately, the implicit assumption of many higher critics is that the Gospels are too complex for the average reader to understand properly, since they mingle fact with myth and imaginative editing. The critics spin out 'secret interpretations that no one knows without a Ph.D.,' snaps Paul Mickey, a conservative at Duke University. Says Father John Navone of the Pontifical Gregorian University in Rome: 'A kind of intellectualist bias has grown up; unless you are aware of the very latest academic theory about the Bible, you might as well not read it.'"[12] So these liberal scholars tell us not to bother with reading the Bible. First, we must consult them, then, presumably, they will tell us what to believe.

If, as Norman Geisler once wrote, unbelief becomes perverse in the face of the extensive evidence for the truth of Christianity, then liberal theologians and their higher criticism are condemned as even more perverse, for they work daily with the Word of God and still reject it.

3. What did the Jesus Seminar conclude about Jesus and His teachings?

How did the 74 Jesus Seminar scholars vote on the genuineness of the words of Jesus? In the most scholarly manner possible: They voted on the authenticity of the words of Jesus by dropping colored balls into a box. In the words of founder and cochair Robert Funk, "Dropping colored beads into a box became the trademark of the Seminar."[13] A red ball meant "Jesus undoubtedly said this or something very like it"; a pink ball meant "Jesus probably said something like this"; gray meant "Jesus did not say this; but the ideas contained in it are close to his own"; a black ball meant "Jesus did not say this; it represents the perspective or content of a later or different tradition."[14]

Only about 18% of Jesus' words "pass" the test and are colored red or pink. Over half are colored black and are therefore, considered false; however, even a good number of the statements of Jesus that pass the test come from the fraudulent, gnostic *Gospel of Thomas*, which the scholars of the JS consider a fifth "Gospel" and more relevant and accurate than the four traditional Gospels.[15] In the four traditional Gospels, only fifteen sayings of Jesus are colored red, and all are short proverb-like sayings or parables. Seventy-five are pink and several hundred black, including *every* single claim Jesus made about Himself. Thus, in the words of the Seminar, fully "eighty-two percent of the words ascribed to Jesus in the gospels were not actually spoken by him."[16]

In other words, Jesus never really believed He would die for the world's sins despite His clear statements: "The Son of Man did not come to be served, but to serve, and to give his life as a ransom for many" (Matthew 26:28); "This is my blood of the covenant, which is poured out for many for the forgiveness of sins" (Matthew 20:28); and "And what shall I say? 'Father, save me from this hour'? No, it was for this very reason that I came to this hour" (John 12:27). Nor did He think He was the Messiah despite John 4:25,26. Here, in response to the woman at the well who said, " 'I know that Messiah (called Christ) is coming,'" we read: "Then Jesus declared, 'I who speak to you am *he*'" (emphasis added). And before the high priest himself Jesus declared under oath that He was the Messiah: "The high priest said to him, 'I charge you under oath by the living God: Tell us if you are the Christ, the Son of God.' 'Yes, it is as you say,' Jesus replied. 'But I say to all of you: In the future you will see the Son of Man sitting at the right hand of the Mighty One and coming on the clouds of heaven'" (Matthew 26:63,64).

In addition, according to liberal theology, Jesus never really claimed to be God, despite statements like the following, "Before Abraham was born, I am" (John 8:58); "I and the Father are one" (John 10:30); and "Anyone who has seen me has seen the Father" (John 14:9). They also say that Jesus never spoke of heaven or hell despite Matthew 25:46: "Then they will go away to eternal punishment, but the righteous to eternal life."

Jesus was not virgin born despite Matthew 1:22,23, which declares: "[The virgin birth of Jesus] took place to fulfill what the Lord had said through the prophet: 'The *virgin* will be with child and will give birth to a son, and they will call him Immanuel'—which means, 'God with us'" (emphasis added).

And of course, they deny that Jesus performed miracles. To the contrary, when John the Baptist was in prison, apparently discouraged, and his disciples told him of all the miracles Jesus was doing, John sent his disciples to ask Jesus whether or not He was the Messiah. Jesus' reply was that the *miracles* He did proved He *was* the Messiah: "At that very time Jesus cured many who had diseases, sicknesses and evil spirits, and gave sight to many who were blind. So he replied to the messengers, 'Go back and report to John what you have seen and heard: The blind receive sight, the lame walk, those who have leprosy are cured, the deaf hear, the dead are raised, and the good news is preached to the poor. Blessed is the man who does not fall away on account of me'" (Luke 7:21-23).

Finally, the Jesus Seminar asks us to believe that Jesus never called for anyone to repent of his or her sins. And Jesus never rose from the dead, despite the unanimous testimony of all four Gospels and the verdict of history. (See our *Knowing the Truth about the Resurrection* [Harvest House, 1996] for more detailed information.)

Welcome to the world of radical biblical scholarship. The fact approximately 15 actual sayings of Jesus were affirmed by the JS (red balls)—and even then not necessarily in each Gospel—reduces Jesus' "authentic" words in the Gospels to less than 6%! In other words, 94% of what is attributed to Jesus in the Gospels has some degree of doubt or is just plain wrong. The Gospel of Mark, for example, had only one single verse out of more than 280 verses spoken by Jesus according to the JS vote. (It was Mark 12:17.) This means that, according to traditional authorship, Mark (or Christian tradition per the JS) misquoted or invented the words of Jesus some 300 times for each time he quoted Jesus correctly. And worse yet (if that were possible), virtually *everything* in the Gospel of

John was voted black! The beloved apostle John had a worse record of accurately recording Jesus' words than Mark.

Everyone can relax now that we know the truth—the Gospels are worthless. We don't have to try to follow Jesus' teachings. To make certain we know it, the JS is now spending its time determining what Jesus never *did* in the Gospels. Next, is their "Call for a Canon Council" to tell us why the books in the Bible (that don't meet with their approval) should be dropped from the canon.[17] So here is the JS order: dismantle Jesus' words, dismantle Jesus' deeds, dismantle the canon. The canon of Scripture, of course, is what *must* go; forget that the canon of Scripture is already established as divinely inspired.[18] Once it is rejected, all the evidence for the historic reliability of the Bible that currently devastates their views won't even matter.

All this only illustrates the bankruptcy of liberal criticism in general. Have critics ever supplied even the smallest amount of evidence to substantiate their incredible assertions? No. Despite thousands of books of nearly worthless speculation, they have never provided even an iota of evidence. All along they have been "arguing in circles and grasping at straws" and "stretching a thin thread thinner."[19]

4. Why should liberal theologians be trusted?

When it comes to their basic worldview and critical methods, liberal theologians should never be trusted. To illustrate, liberals assume, *a priori*, the Gospel writers were so overladen with "Christianizing" myths and propaganda that their writings are useless for determining who Jesus really was and therefore, are essentially valueless as accurate historical documents. If what these scholars say is true, Christianity is not just a false religion, it is a worthless religion and a fraud of the worst sort. One is tempted to think that having people arrive at such a conclusion is perhaps the real motive underlying the works of many of these scholars. Why do scholars spend so much time and effort attempting to *disprove* what is so obviously a falsehood to begin with? (Hint: Maybe it's because they think the Gospel portrayal of Jesus might really be true but want to convince themselves otherwise. Sort of like the TV narrator who said, "Perhaps the most fearful thing about the Christian hell is that it might be true."[20])

It doesn't take a rocket scientist to determine from the New Testament accounts that Jesus claimed to be God and that He said His words would never pass away. Nor does it take a Nobel prize winner or a Ph.D. in New Testament Studies from Harvard to ascertain, with a relatively small amount of study, that the New Testament documents are historically accurate and that Jesus rose physically from the dead. What *is* noteworthy is the tremendous amount of legitimate scholarship the rationalistic theologians, liberals, and skeptics completely disregard in order to maintain their own biases.

The kind of audacity displayed in the Jesus Seminar, which actually votes on the accuracy and reliability of Jesus' statements and assumes that only critical scholars have the right to judge New Testament reliability, represents the height of insolence (Jesus is, after all, God incarnate!) As to knowledge of New Testament reliability, the informed Christian is actually *better* educated than these scholars whose rationalistic, skeptical assumptions leave them in a hopeless muddle or speaking nonsense, uncertain what to believe. As one critic noted, "If a vote were taken on the usefulness of the Jesus Seminar, is there any doubt what the outcome would be?"[21] What bold arrogance! One can only wonder what Jesus Himself would think of all this—especially since He was the one who promised us: "Heaven and earth will pass away, but my words will *never* pass away" (Matthew 24:35, emphasis added). Is there a member of the JS or liberal theology anywhere who is willing to predict that he or she will rise from the dead, and then *do it* as proof of the truth of his or her claim?

We think that most liberal biblical scholars, who have done so much to damage the cause and credibility of Christianity can hardly be seen as objective theologians honestly searching for the "real" Jesus. After all, the real Jesus has been clearly present in the Scriptures for 2,000 years. Instead, these liberals should be viewed as self-serving ideologues (indeed, hypocrites, if they claim to be Christian) at best and, at worst, as enemies of the Christian faith. No other perspective can do them justice. Discontent to keep their destructive views to themselves, they actively seek to persuade others not to trust in the biblical picture of Jesus.[22] And they are highly successful. Their "new view of Christ that denies His supremacy is gaining followers all over the world."[23] The

Jesus Seminar releases its findings just before Easter and Christmas in a calculated attempt to target the public at the best possible time to secure maximum exposure for their erroneous views.

Although the JS speaks of the supposed "assured results of critical scholarship,"[24] their critical apparatus only serves to destroy objective historical inquiry. The JS makes these inaccurate conclusions regarding Jesus:

> The gospel writers overlaid the tradition of [Jesus'] sayings and parables with their own [inaccurate] "memories" of Jesus.... The Jesus of the gospels is an *imaginative* theological *construct*.... The gospels are...narratives in which the memory of Jesus is embellished by *mythic* elements that express the church's faith in him, and by plausible *fictions* that enhance the telling of the gospel story for first-century listeners who knew about divine men and miracle workers firsthand.... The figure in [the Apostle's] creed is a *mythical* or heavenly figure.... espoused by the apostle Paul, who did not know the historical Jesus. For Paul, the Christ was to be understood as a dying/rising lord, symbolized in baptism... of the type he knew from the hellenistic mystery religions. In Paul's theological scheme, Jesus the man played no essential role.... Christian conviction eventually overwhelms Jesus: he is [falsely] made to confess what Christians had come to believe.[25]

Of course, the liberals often claim they are unbiased scholars doing first-rate scholarship. For example, in the words of the JS, which labels its "translation" the Scholars Version (SV):

> The Scholars Version is free of ecclesiastical and religious control, unlike other major translations into English.... "The Scholars Version is authorized by scholars" and "The Fellows of the Seminar are critical scholars. To be a *critical* scholar means to make empirical, factual evidence—evidence open to confirmation by independent, neutral observers—the controlling factor in historical judgments. Noncritical scholars are those who put dogmatic considerations first and insist that the factual evidence confirm theological premises. Critical scholars adopt the principle of methodological skepticism: accept only what passes the rigorous tests of the rules of evidence.... The scholarship represented by the Fellows of the Jesus Seminar is the kind that has come to prevail in all the great universities of the world.... Public attack on the members of the Seminar

is commonplace, coming especially from those who lack academic credentials."[26]

What the members of the JS won't recognize is that it is the conservative view of Scripture that "passes the rigorous tests of the rules of evidence"—not their historical distortions. This has already been established by a great weight of evangelical and nonevangelical scholarship. They also don't seem to recognize they put their own "dogmatic considerations first and insist the factual evidence confirm [to their] theological premises." Therefore, the liberal quest for "the historical Jesus" can only terminate as theological road kill along the path to, presumably, not heaven. A *Newsweek* article even commented, "After 150 years of scholarly search, there are signs that the quest for the 'historical' Jesus has reached a dead end. There have been no new data on the person of Jesus since the gospels were written."[27] The major reason a critical search exists at all is because many people don't want to believe what the Gospels clearly state about Jesus. The real problem is that the critics don't want to believe in Jesus. As we demonstrated in *Ready with an Answer* (Harvest House, 1997), *Knowing the Truth About the Reliability of the Bible*, and other works, the problem is not the quality of the evidence in substantiating biblical Christianity and its documents as historically reliable. That evidence is easily available to anyone who seeks it. Indeed, if the Gospels are so obviously fraudulent, it is unlikely the very term Gospel would ever come to be so widely accepted as synonymous with "a thing one may safely believe."

When one looks at evangelical scholarship in, for example, the six-volume *Gospel Perspectives* (Sheffield, JSOT Press, 1986), a ten-year project by an international team of scholars, or N.T. Wright's projected five-volume work, *Christian Origins and the Question of God*, or critiques of the JS such as Michael Wilkins and J.P. Moreland's *Jesus Under Fire* and Gregory Boyd's *Cynic, Sage or Son of God*? one finds a clear and unambiguous refutation of what the liberals are doing as well as objective, scholarly defenses of New Testament Christianity. The purpose of *Gospel Perspectives*, for example, was, according to the series preface: "to provide answers to the questions of historicity which will stand up to serious academic scrutiny and will provide some help for those who are perplexed by scholarly disagreement."[28]

When the harmful conclusions of the Jesus Seminar are broadcast nationwide—and indeed worldwide—it's not difficult to understand why Christians who believe in the Bible are so upset by these so-called biblical scholars' approach to Scripture. The JS distortions are being disseminated everywhere. In the past decade the Seminar participants have actively sought to publicize their views. Indeed, it would be difficult to find a newspaper in America that hasn't done a story on the Seminar over the past decade.

It is perhaps no exaggeration to say that the JS has had more impact in North America at a popular level than any other scholarly discussion of Jesus in the last 200 years. Thus, "the growing popularity of this paradigm should be of significant concern for all Christians and not just New Testament scholars. If it was ever excusable for evangelical laypeople to ignore the latest trends in New Testament scholarship, it is no longer."[29] (See also the sources in 30-45, esp. note 38.)

5. *What are liberal theologians responsible for?*

Lest we think this is all just academic debating, consider the tragic event relayed by William Lane Craig in *The Son Rises*. He recalls the incident of a retired pastor "who in his spare time began to study the thought of certain modern theologians." This pastor believed that their great learning was superior to his own and concluded that their views must be correct. "He understood clearly what that meant for him: his whole life and ministry had been based on a bundle of lies. He committed suicide." Dr. Craig comments, quite correctly, "I believe that modern theologians must answer to God for that man's death. One cannot make statements on such matters without accepting part of the responsibility for the consequences."[46] (The incident referred specifically to the liberals' denial of the resurrection but is applicable generally.) Indeed, "We are not overstating it when we say that these are life and death issues. . . . If Jesus is who he claimed to be and who his followers declare him to be, then we are not dealing simply with academic questions. We are instead dealing with the most important questions of the modern person's daily life and eternal destiny."[47]

Millions of people in the modern world have accepted as "gospel" what these critics believe about the Bible. They are, after all, "experts"—and as theologians they should know. But how many people have they turned away from the true gospel? How many of the redeemed in the church have they confused?[48]

At the "John Ankerberg Show," we receive numerous letters from Muslims, Mormons and members of other religious cults, and secular critics who attempt to show us the error of our ways regarding biblical inerrancy and authority. Their arguments appeal almost exclusively to the "findings" of liberal theologians and higher critics.

Few things are as culpable as theologians, who should be the very defenders of eternal truth, subverting the truth to uphold their own biases.

6. What are the major problems with the Jesus Seminar?

Three of the key belief errors made by the Jesus Seminar (JS) are: 1) its conclusions represent a consensus of modern scholarship; 2) it ignores deliberate skepticism and bias, which are entirely without justification (for example, its agenda to discredit people's trust in the Gospels, which have been established as historically reliable); and 3) it fails to recognize the serious or fatal philosophical and methodological flaws that undermine its own conclusions.

First, the truth is that the JS does not represent a consensus of New Testament (NT) or biblical scholarship, even if we entirely discard conservative, evangelical scholarship. The JS view clearly represents a minority view: "The Jesus Seminar does not reflect either responsible scholarship or critical consensus, and it is a pity that many in the media have allowed themselves to be deceived by its claims to the contrary. . . . Although this work repeatedly claims to reflect a consensus of modern scholars, this claim is simply false, even if one leaves all evangelical scholars to one side."[49] Also, the views of 70 critics can hardly be considered representative of the 7,000 members of the Society of Biblical Literature (SBL) or thousands of others:

> Perhaps the most striking feature of *The Five Gospels* is how out of touch it is even with mainline scholarship. In fact, a major movement among New Testament critics has generated what has been dubbed "the third quest" for the historical Jesus. This quest has been far more

optimistic than its predecessors in claiming that substantial amounts of material about what Jesus said and did can be recovered from the canonical Gospels. Indeed, two of the major contributors to this quest—James Charlesworth of Princeton and E.P. Sanders of Duke—agree that "the dominant view today seems to be that we can know pretty well what Jesus was out to accomplish, that we can know a lot about what he said, and that those two things make sense within the world of first-century Judaism." It is this final clause that the JS virtually ignores. Their Jesus does not make sense in the world of Judaism.[50]

Second, as we have indicated, the biases of members of the JS are clearly present in their writings.

> No other scholarship on Jesus, or on any other religious teacher for that matter, imposes such stringent restrictions. No sage in the history of the world is so limited in the forms of speech he or she could possibly have employed—not Buddha, not Confucius, not Mohammed, not even the modern avant-garde writers like Franz Kafka, with whom Jesus is often favorably compared in these circles.... Whatever else modern scholarship may disagree on, there is widespread consensus that Jesus must be read against the historical-cultural milieu of his world, a milieu that was above all Jewish. This the Jesus Seminar simply does not do.[51]

Further, Seminar cochair John Dominic Crossan—

> seeks to undercut the credibility of the Gospel accounts of Jesus' burial and resurrection by means of a general analysis of the Gospel texts and traditions that is so bizarre and contrived that the overwhelming majority of the New Testament critics find it wholly implausible. It is sobering to think that it is this sort of idiosyncratic speculation that thousands of lay readers of magazines like *Time* have come to believe represents the best of contemporary New Testament scholarship concerning the historical Jesus.[52]

Crossan's methods and conjectures in, for example, *The Historical Jesus* are so ersatz he asks at one point, "Is an understanding of the historical Jesus of any permanent relevance to Christianity itself?"[53] He also admits, "*Historical Jesus research* is becoming something of a scholarly bad joke."[54] Indeed, no better illustration is found than in Crossan's own book.

Third, there are philosophical and methodological flaws that are either false or refute the JS's own conclusions.

One of the dominant premises of the JS is a philosophical naturalism that, although fake, by definition supports the critical agenda of the JS:

> The Jesus Seminar has an agenda other than the academic one—an agenda for the people of the church.... They want to liberate the people of the church from the "dark ages of theological tyranny" by liberating Jesus. As Robert Funk, cofounder of the Jesus Seminar states, "We want to liberate Jesus. The only Jesus most people know is the mythic one. They don't want the real Jesus, they want the one they can worship. The cultic Jesus." ... The members of the Jesus Seminar are committed to a strict philosophical naturalism....
>
> Philosophical naturalism is an expression of an epistemology (i.e., a theory of knowledge and justified or warranted belief) known as scientism.... Everything outside of science is a matter of mere belief and subjective opinion, of which rational assessment is impossible. Applied to the question of the historical origins of Christianity ... we can no longer believe in a biblical worldview with its miracles, demons, and supernatural realities.[55]

This scientism can be seen in *The Five Gospels*. For instance, in the claim that "the Christ creed and dogma... can no longer command the assent of those who have seen the heavens through Galileo's telescope. The old deities and demons were swept from the skies. ... [Science has] dismantled the mythological abodes of the gods and Satan, and bequeathed us secular heavens."[56]

But scientism itself has long been discredited:

> It is well past time to rest content with the politically correct, unjustified assertions of scientism and philosophical naturalism. University libraries are filled with books that show the weaknesses of these views, and the fellows of the Jesus Seminar show virtually no indication that they have so much as interacted with the arguments they contain, much less have they refuted their claims.[57]

In other words,

> To the Jesus Seminar, the historical Jesus of Nazareth *by definition* must be a nonsupernatural Jesus.... The Jesus Seminar Fellows have clearly aligned themselves with Strauss: "the distinction between the historical Jesus ... and the Christ of faith" is deemed the first pillar of "scholarly wisdom" and "modern biblical criticism." For

them, Jesus' resurrection from the dead is not a live option even to be considered as a possible explanation for the relevant data; a naturalistic explanation, no matter how outlandish, will *always* be preferred over a supernaturalistic explanation.... The bottom line is that what the Jesus Seminar calls the first pillar of scholarly wisdom is nothing more than a philosophical prejudice that actually impedes a fair assessment of the evidence relevant to the resurrection of Jesus.[58]

Another false assumption of the Jesus Seminar includes the belief that the authors of the Gospels can't be trusted because they were Christians. However, does anyone ever fault the research findings of medical doctors simply because they are physicians?

Examples of the JS methodological flaws are seen in their use of their many "rules of evidence" and "criteria of authenticity" standards which they employ to allegedly separate out the "real" teachings of Jesus.[59] For example, "The Jesus Seminar formulated and adopted 'rules of evidence' to guide its assessment of gospel traditions. Rules of evidence are standards by which evidence is presented and evaluated in court."[60] But the JS claim to impartiality and using legal standards of evidence is highly misleading. The truth is that their "rules" are frequently irrelevant and/or *incorporate their own biases* against the text so that *applying* the rules only proves the critical conclusions already held. For example, their context rule *assumes,* without justification, that the Gospel writers invented new narrative contexts for the sayings of Jesus.[61] Their commentary rule *assumes,* without justification, that the Gospel writers revised Jesus' sayings to conform to their own particularist views.[62] The "false attribution rule" *assumes,* without justification, that "the evangelists frequently attribute their own statements to Jesus."[63] Their "rules of evidence" *assume,* without justification, that the Gospels as we have them are inventions and myths.

Unfortunately for the JS, however, an unbiased application of other critical "criteria of authenticity" *support* traditional views:

> We have summarized the evidence for the historicity of Jesus' resurrection. As one reflects on this evidence, it is striking how successfully the historical material undergirding the physical resurrection of Jesus passes the received tests of authenticity employed by the Fellows of the Jesus Seminar. Evans has recently argued

that the same criteria used to establish the authenticity of the sayings of Jesus can also be used to establish the miraculous deeds of Jesus.[64]

As Craig Blomberg (Ph.D., University of Aberdeen, professor of New Testament at Denver Seminary) points out,

> The four criteria of authenticity most commonly employed in the search for authentic gospel material are the criteria of multiple attestation or forms, of Palestinian environment or language, of dissimilarity, and of coherence. . . . Using these criteria, even the person who is suspicious of the gospel tradition may come to accept a large percentage of it as historically accurate. . . . In fact, patient application of the criteria of authenticity can itself eventually lead one to accept virtually all the gospel tradition. . . . [Thus,] whether by giving the gospels the benefit of the doubt which all narratives of purportedly historical events merit or by approaching them with an initial suspicion in which every detail must satisfy the criteria of authenticity, the verdict should remain the same. The gospels may be accepted as trustworthy accounts of what Jesus did and said.[65]

The *real* issue has nothing to do with the objective and judicial application of rules of evidence, since these disprove JS claims and establish the Bible, as Montgomery and others have shown.[66] The real issue for the JS is to be rid of the biblical Jesus:

> In fact, one can suggest that Christology is the *real* issue in the debate over many sayings, much more so than history or the objective application of abstract criteria. In an almost circular kind of way, a saying is accepted because it reflects a certain circumscribed Christology formed on an impression not created by the consistent application of the criteria, but by the preconceived, limited Christology. . . . There is good reason to defend the authenticity of the ransom concept in the ministry of Jesus himself, even on the basis of the criterion for authenticity the Seminar uses! As one examines these criteria individually, it becomes clear that even by these more discriminating standards a case can be made for the major redemptive and Christological themes of Jesus' ministry. The judgments of the Seminar are suspect even by their own limiting standards.[67]

The JS scholars also violate their own stated safeguard, which they claim all responsible scholars practice:

"The last temptation is to create Jesus in our own image, to martial the facts to support preconceived convictions. This fatal pitfall has prompted the Jesus Seminar to adopt as its final general rule of evidence: *Beware of finding a Jesus entirely congenial to you.*"[68] Yet the very next sentence reads, "Eighty-two percent of the words ascribed to Jesus in the gospels were not actually spoken by him. . . . "[69]

When they condescendingly disparage conservative Christians as "far right fundamentalists," "latter-day inquisitors," and "witch-hunters," and then claim "their reading of who Jesus was rests on the shifting sands of their own theological constructions," one can only stand in wonder at the hubris.[70]

One reads with further astonishment, "The evidence provided by the written gospels is hearsay evidence. Hearsay evidence is secondhand evidence. . . . None of [the Gospel authors] was an ear or eyewitness of the words and events he records."[71] But this is exactly what the New Testament writers claim—to be ear and eyewitnesses: "That . . . which we have heard, which we have seen with our eyes, which we have looked at and our hands have touched—this we proclaim. . . . We proclaim to you what we have seen and heard" (1 John 1:1,3, cf., Luke 1:2; Hebrews 2:3; 1 Peter 5:1; John 3:11; 5:36; 19:35; 21:24; Acts 2:32; 3:15; 4:33; 5:32; 10:39; 26:26; 1 John 4:14; 5:9,10; 3 John 1:2; Luke 24:48).

By now it is obvious the scholars of the JS care nothing for objective historical inquiry or truth. If they did, they could never make such a statement as that just quoted above. The "Dictionary of more Terms" concluding *The Five Gospels* defines "critical" scholarship as meaning "to exercise careful, considered judgment."[72] This is something JS members fail to do.

Even the author of the Easter article published by *Newsweek*, hardly a conservative theological think tank, saw through their agenda: "They apply the critical tools of today: text chopping, psychological speculation and colleague-bashing. And then they take leaps of faith, often of their own creation. Of the dozens of recent books denying the resurrection stories, many are written by liberal scholars who think the time has come to replace the 'cultic' Jesus of Christian worship with the 'real' Jesus unearthed by academic research. Theirs is not disinterested historical investigation but scholarship with a frankly missionary purpose: by reconstructing the life of Jesus they hope to show that belief in the bodily resurrection of Jesus is a burden to the Christian faith and deflects attention from his role as a social reformer. . . . In short, modern psychology reduces the Risen Christ to a series of interpsychic experiences that produced in the disciples a renewed sense of missionary zeal and spiritual self-confidence."[73]

Not only is there not much new in the liberals' approach (similar conclusions having been presented for the last 150 years by previous critics), their scholarship per se cannot bear its own weight. A *Christianity Today* article mentions that in *The Real Jesus*, Luke Timothy Johnson points out that these scholars are naive in how they approach historical sources, in their understanding of what history is and can achieve, and in the nature and limits of historical knowledge. Indeed, "the scholarship that undergirds the Jesus Seminar and similar enterprises is based on wild speculation and minuscule evidence."[74] In the words of biblical scholar Dr. Gary Habermas, "Seldom do the Jesus Seminar Fellows provide *reasons* for their opinions or otherwise vindicate their own worldview."[75]

7. What is the enigmatic "Q"? Where is it?

To illustrate the "wild speculation and minuscule evidence" referred to earlier by Johnson, consider the alleged collection of Jesus' sayings termed "Q" (supposedly used by Matthew, Mark, and Luke). Liberal scholars such as Burton Mack, in *Who Wrote the New Testament?: The Making of the Christian Myth* (1995), are now speaking of Q1, Q2, Q3, and Q4, which, Johnson correctly points out, is preposterous and explains "why so much of contemporary New Testament scholarship is viewed with derision by mainstream historians. The entire edifice is 'a house of cards.' . . . Pull out one element and the whole construction crumbles."[76]

"Q" illustrates the quagmire scholars get themselves into when they are unwilling to take the biblical text at face value—even though there is every good reason to do so. "Q" doesn't even *exist*; yet literally *hundreds of thousands* of hours have been consumed dissecting this purely imaginary text! This is illustrated in the "International Q Project's" database research, which contains, for example, a 90-page, single-spaced analysis of a *single* verse from Matthew that was ultimately decided *not* to be "Q"! The kind of scholarly speculation and/or nonsense represented by "Q" is almost maddening. Why emphasize the detailed study of something that doesn't exist, when what *does* exist is authentic and accurate? Yet the "Q" project intends to publish over sixty 300-page volumes painstakingly evaluating an imaginary text! Each 300-page volume will deal with about 100 words from "Q"; per volume, that's 3 pages of scholarly analysis and discussion for every nonexistent word of "Q."[77]

Why do critics demand we reject as myth the "inventive imaginations" of the early Christians in their portrait of Jesus, but then turn around and demand we accept their own fictitious reconstructions as literal "Gospel"?

John Wenham has had a distinguished academic career as vice principal of Tyndale Hall, Bristol, lecturer in New Testament Greek at Bristol University, and warden of Latimer House, Oxford. He is the author of such important works as *Christ and the Bible* and *The Goodness of God*. In *Redating Matthew, Mark and Luke*, in which he dates the synoptics at 40, 45 and 54 respectively, he illustrates the quandary of those who employ obviously biased higher-critical methods rather than an objective and more fair scholarship that takes all the known factual data into account. Wenham quotes M.D. Goulder who writes, "Not tens but hundreds of thousands of pages have been wasted by authors on this Synoptic Problem [the likenesses and differences between the first three gospels] not paying attention to errors of method." Wenham goes on to comment that "much of the argumentation is worth very little, because so many of the arguments are reversible: they can be argued either way with approximately equal cogency."[78] Thus, "the view that Matthew and Luke independently used Mark and a lost source Q is still held as a working hypothesis by most scholars, but with decreasing confidence."[79]

He says of "Q," with a highly enlightening illustration:

> When we try to put the Q-theory to the test, the matter is of course complicated by the fact that we have no text of Q to work with.... S. Petrie in his *Novum Testamentum* 3 (1959) article, " 'Q' Is Only What You Make It" has shown this in a colourful way. He speaks of the 'exasperating contradictoriness' of scholarly views as to its nature:

> "Q" is a single document; it is a composite document, incorporating earlier sources; it is used in different redactions; it is more than one document. The original language of "Q" is Greek; the original language is Aramaic; it is used in different translations. "Q" is the Matthean Logia; it is not the Matthean Logia. "Q" has a definite shape; it is no more than an amorphous collection of fragments. "Q" is a gospel; it is not a gospel. "Q" includes the Crucifixion story; it does not include the Crucifixion story. "Q" consists wholly of sayings and there is no narrative; it includes some narrative. All of "Q" is preserved in Matthew and Luke; not all of it is preserved; it is better preserved in Luke. Matthew's order is the correct order; Luke's is the correct order; neither order is correct. "Q" is used by Mark; it is not used by Mark.[80]

It seems obvious the critical scholars have used inventive theories like "Q" to make Jesus into an image they are comfortable with—whether political revolutionary, proto-feminist, mystic, cynic, and so forth. Jesus' death and resurrection play no role in Q's understanding of salvation which is more gnostic than orthodox. We further see "Q" appropriated by the JS "in their ongoing enterprise of 'dismantling the church's canon.'"[81] As Mack argues, "The remarkable thing about the people of Q is that they were not Christians. They did not think of Jesus as a Messiah. They did not regard his death as a . . . saving event. . . . They did not imagine that he had been raised from the dead. . . . "[82]

Every other image of Jesus is acceptable to critics except the one in the New Testament. As a *Christianity Today* article pointed out, their answer to who Jesus is seems to "be almost anything *but* the risen Christ worshipped by believers around the world."[83] Indeed, for the JS, "This Jesus is more Gnostic—concerned primarily to impart true knowledge—than anything orthodox Christianity has ever accepted. Today we might call it 'New Age.' But given the JS's stated goal of discrediting orthodox Christianity and going beyond mainstream scholarship (despite their repeated claims that they represent a consensus), this conclusion should not be surprising."[84]

By now, the reason for their conclusions should be obvious: If we accept the real Jesus of history, the Jesus in the New Testament, then He is indeed our Lord, Savior, and Judge. He is not someone we may trifle with but one we must bow to as our Sovereign. We may sit in judgment upon Him now, but it is *He* who will judge *us* at the last day. Since the human heart, in its rebellion against God, prefers anything other than this, the almost desperate nature of the offensive "scholarship" to formulate a new Jesus is understandable. Once the biblical Jesus is safely disposed of we need not worry about His claims on our lives or the possibility of our own judgments in the next life for rejecting Him now. Perhaps more than any other factor, this explains why liberal scholars strain at such unjustified assumptions in their treatment of the biblical text.

8. What should be rejected—the New Testament (NT) or the liberal critics?

> "Jesus was not the first Christian. However he is often made to talk like a Christian by his devoted followers" (*The Five Gospels*, p. 24).

Should we reject what the NT says about Jesus as the liberals would have us do? Or should we reject the liberals' conclusions? The evidence demands we reject the liberals. Our companion volume, *Knowing the Truth About the Reliability of the Bible* proves this.

For now, consider another statement from a *Newsweek* article which sets the tone for the following discussion. It further illustrates the current bias against the New Testament: "Unfortunately, apart from what is found in Scripture, there is little that one can say about the identity of Jesus."[85] Besides this statement being so obviously false,[86] on what historical, rational basis can the words of the New Testament writers be rejected? Why this unwavering bias against the writings of nine men who have, for 2,000 years, been proven to be honest, historical reporters? Has even a single argument against their accuracy withstood the test of time? No. In the Gospels we have four accounts: Matthew and John, written by eyewitnesses who spent three years with Jesus and knew Him intimately, and Mark and Luke, based on information from the apostles (Peter and Paul, respectively) and written with great care by men whose integrity is unassailable.

These four accounts have been subjected to the most vigorous criticism for 2,000 years by some of the world's best and most critical intellects who have yet to make a case. The writers themselves declare that they were either eyewitnesses to the events recorded or that they took pains to research and write with care and accuracy exactly what happened. In composing his biography of Jesus, the apostle Luke told Theophilus, for example, "I myself have carefully investigated everything from the beginning . . . so that you may know the certainty of the things you have been taught" (Luke 1:3,4). In referring to his entire Gospel, the apostle John ended his biography with these words, "This is the disciple who testifies to these things and who wrote them down. We *know* that his testimony is true" (John 21:24). He also states, "The man who saw it has given testimony, and his testimony is true. He knows that he tells the truth, and he testifies so that you also may believe" (John 19:35). John was so confident in the accuracy of his Gospel that he made these bold statements publicly—even to those most eager to disprove them. The apostle Peter, from whom Mark received the information for his Gospel, also asserted to eyewitness testimony: "We did not follow cleverly invented stories when we told you about the power and coming of our Lord Jesus Christ, but we were *eyewitnesses* of his majesty" (2 Peter 1:16). Peter's comment could almost be considered a personal rebuke to the participants in the Jesus Seminar. Or perhaps the members of the JS would prefer to listen to the words of Albert Einstein, who wrote of the Jesus of the Gospels in response to liberalism, "No myth is filled with such life."[87]

As noted biblical scholar F.F. Bruce remarks, "There is, I imagine, no body of literature in the world that has been exposed to the stringent analytical study that the four gospels have sustained for the past 200 years. This is not something to be regretted; it is something to be accepted with satisfaction. Scholars today who treat the gospels as credible historical documents do so in the full light of analytical study, not by closing their minds to it."[88] What more could the Christian ask for? What more does the critic want?

The writings of the Gospels themselves bear the ring of truth by what they report and the manner by which they report it. Yet, we are told that these writings are not to be trusted. And on what basis? Largely because of the widely disseminated, entirely false conclusions of the liberal theologians.

Here is the real truth. If we discard the Gospels as accurate history, then, because of the basis upon which we can document their historicity, we must literally throw out every other ancient historical document. And which of the critics and liberal scholars are willing to do that? When it comes down to it, not one. As Dr. Montgomery recalled on "The John Ankerberg Show":

> Last week we mentioned a debate that I had some years ago with Professor Stroll at the University of British Columbia. Professor Stroll said that the documents of the New Testament were simply not adequate to get a picture of Jesus. I offered evidence to show that these documents are the best attested documents of the classical world. I said, "If you want to give up Jesus Christ, you first of all have got to dump your knowledge of the classical world." Professor Stroll said, "Fine. I will throw out the classical world." At which point the head of the classics department got up and said, "Good Lord, Avrum, not *that*!"
>
> You can't just toss out Greco-Roman antiquity because you don't want to face the documents that present Jesus Christ. Last week we went over these documents and we showed that these documents are sound historical materials for understanding who Jesus actually was.[89]

As Dr. Gregory A. Boyd (Yale University Divinity School; Ph.D. Princeton Theological Seminary) correctly points out, "The most compelling argument against any revisionist account of the historical Jesus is not the exposition of its internal weaknesses, as crucial as that is. It is, rather, the *positive* evidence for the reliability of the New Testament's portrait of Christ."[90]

Here is the real Jesus, authenticated by the New Testament. He declares: "I am the light of the world. Whoever follows me will never walk in darkness, but will have the light of life" (John 8:12). "I am the way, and the truth and the life. No one comes to the Father except through me" (John 14:6). "I am the resurrection and the life. He who believes in me will live, even though he dies" (John 11:25).

Jesus commanded a people to love Him in the exact same way that they loved God—with all their heart, soul, and mind (Matthew 22:37,38). Jesus said that God the Holy Spirit would bear witness of Him and glorify Him (John 16:13,14). He said that to know Him was to know God (John 14:7). To receive Him was to receive God (Matthew 10:40). To honor Him was to honor God (John 5:23). To believe in Him was to believe in God

(John 12:44,45; 14:1). To see Him was to see God (John 8:19; 14:7). To deny Him was to deny God (1 John 2:23). To hate Him was to hate God (John 15:23).

In Matthew 25, Jesus said that He would return at the end of the world to judge every person who ever lived. He would personally raise *all* the dead, and all the nations would be gathered before Him! He would sit on His throne of glory and judge and separate the people one from another as a shepherd does the sheep from the goats (Matthew 25:31-46; see also John 5:25-34). Just as clearly, Jesus taught that every person's eternal destiny depended upon how he or she treated Him (John 8:24; Matthew 10:32).

> On the lips of anyone else the claims of Jesus would appear to be evidence of gross egomania, for Jesus clearly implies that the entire world revolves around himself and that the fate of all men is dependent on their acceptance or rejection of him.... There seem to be only two possible ways of interpreting the totalitarian nature of the claims of Jesus. Either we must assume that Jesus was deluded and unstable with unusual delusions of grandeur, or we are faced with the realization that Jesus is truly One who speaks with divine authority, who actually divided all of history into B.C.–A.D., and whose rejection or acceptance determines the fate of men.[91]

All these statements and many more like them, leave us little choice. Either Jesus was who He said He was—God incarnate—or He was absolutely crazy. But who believes that?

What the members of the JS are unwilling to concede is precisely what will write their own epitaph—the fact that "there is a huge volume of scholarship to support the picture of Jesus that Matthew, Mark, Luke and John portray."[92] In time, the research of the Jesus Seminar, and indeed, all liberal, critical biblical "scholarship," will be relegated to the "circular files" of rationalistic, historical skepticism for the simple reason that they "evince a prejudice against the New Testament documents that can only be described as historically irresponsible."[93] An article in *Time* magazine even questioned what the final outcome of the JS and the search for the historical Jesus would be four or five years from now: "Their areas of agreement, thus far, have largely been in the negative, and their respective rescued Jesuses vary considerably." Crossan himself thinks that in the end "there could be hopeless disagreement."[94]

What other conclusion could one logically expect from the kind of irresponsible scholarship, subjectivism, and biased historical research we find in the Jesus Seminar?[95 (cf. 96-99)]

The conclusions drawn by higher criticism of the JS are demonstrably false and yet maintained in spite of this. It is logically impossible to believe the basic assumption of any criticism which, in effect, attributes to a first-century, scattered Christian community the kind of creative power to invent the Jesus Christ of the New Testament. This is either unbelievable, absurd, or both:

> With regard to the discourses attributed to Jesus, it should at once be realized that a community cannot create such sayings. We know from experience that a saying must come originally from an individual. A community can only adopt, transmit, and preserve a saying, but the saying itself must first exist. Now the sayings attributed to Jesus in the gospels are by common consent of a singular nobility, loftiness, and power; elevated in character and style. If it be held that in some way the Christian community originated these discourses and statements, then it must follow, as scholar Burton Scott Easton argues, that the Palestinian church either had in its midst a single, brilliant thinker "from whom the sayings all proceeded, but whose name and very existence has disappeared from history—something well-nigh unthinkable—or else there were a number of gifted individuals all fired with the same superlative genius and all endowed with the same exquisite style—an even more difficult conception."
>
> The simple fact is that there is not the slightest indication in New Testament or secular history of the existence of such an anonymous, dynamic, prophetic leader, who would surely be greater and wiser even than ancient Solomon; or of a group of such leaders, gifted with the capacity of creating original discourses such as are found in the gospels. The only plausible explanation for these sayings is that they originated, as the evangelists declare, with Jesus; the life situation from which they stem is assuredly to be found in Jesus Himself.[100]

Indeed, the more we carefully examine higher criticism, the more difficult it is to accept its conclusions. It is nonsense to really believe that all the teachings of Jesus in the New Testament are myths concocted from the inventive imagination of early Christian believers. Or that they were then uncritically accepted by other

Christian people everywhere—even though these stories were all easily discerned hoaxes. Early Christians could check out the details of the Gospels by talking to those who were eyewitnesses of Jesus' ministry. If what the critics say *were* true, there never would have been a Christianity to begin.

In the end, our only options are to believe in the foolishness of a critical methodology that invents myths or in the soundness of conservative biblical scholarship that has established its methods and conclusions. No other choices remain. Unfortunately, some people in the church think it is proper for Christians to use higher critical methods.

SECTION II

Higher Criticism, the Bible, and the Church

9. Is higher critical methodology necessarily opposed to God and His Word?

The father of the historical critical approach to the Bible, or higher criticism, is usually acknowledged to be Johann Salomo Semler in the late 1700s. The search for the "historical" Jesus per se began with Hermann Samuel Reimarus (1694-1768), who assumed the real words of Jesus in the New Testament could be distinguished from what the Gospel authors made Him say. Reimarus believed the Gospel writers were guilty of intentional, deliberate fabrication.[101] Semler may have been influenced by Reimarus. As Eugene F. Klug points out, Semler's method "was really a revolt against miracles and the supernatural in general, and against heaven in particular."[102] In fact, we can see this revolt as a dominant theme throughout the history of higher criticism right up to the present. And, despite its tremendous influence, higher criticism has always suffered from the same fatal flaws: skepticism, rationalism, and scientific naturalism.

What the critics of the Bible seem not to have internalized is that the individual steps that are followed in any critical method can only be as useful or valid as the assumptions which underlie them. If the assumptions are false, the conclusions based on them must also be false.

Which radical scholar accepts the supernatural? Yet miracles and the supernatural are inherently a part of what God does in history because God is a supernatural being. The Bible is checkered with miracles from beginning to end, from creation, the fall, and the flood to the exodus, conquest, prophets, captivity/return to the Gospels, Acts, epistles, and Revelation.

Which radical scholar accepts a first-century date of the New Testament and the traditional authorship of the Gospels? Which radical scholar believes Jesus is Lord and Savior? In using the methodology of unbelief, it is hardly surprising that the end results in unbelief.

As Eugene Klug writes in the foreword of *The End of the Historical-Critical Method*, "Historical-critical methodology cannot be claimed as a neutral discipline. It holds sway in 'scientific' theology pretty much as evolutionism rules the scientific disciplines. Theories multiply, often with total disdain for the facts, at times even though the facts contradict the conclusions. People finally believe what they want to believe."[103]

A reporter for *Time* magazine, Richard N. Ostling concludes his article, "Who Was Jesus?" by mentioning the English moderate Canon Harvey recalling a mentor pointing out that in any investigation of history, "If you tear up the only evidence you've got, you can say anything you like." Ostling comments, "That is not a bad one-sentence summary of what has happened to higher biblical criticism."[104] As Klug points out, this entire process was doomed to failure from the start because it destroyed the very thing it was seeking to dissect—the Scriptures.[105]

In essence, "a critical method of Bible interpretation can produce only Bible-critical propositions. This is true even in those instances where the historical-critical method confirms Bible propositions. For the justification and authority of the outcome are still established by the critical scholar himself and, due to the method, cannot come only out of Scripture. The historical-critical method, in its actual application, has become an impenetrable screen which simply does not allow certain statements anymore, even though they may be proved a thousand times in the experience of believers. This is not evil intent but the helplessness into which a falsely selected method blunders."[106] Gerhard Maier is absolutely correct when he describes higher criticism as "a truly dictatorial regime in theology."[107] In this role it matches the stature of evolutionary theory in the sciences. Long overdue, it is time to recognize what negative historical criticism truly is: "an uncritical and unjustified denigration of the Biblical text" and a "godless technique that eroded the Word of God itself."[108]

Semler may have believed that "the root of the evil (in theology) is the interchangeable use of the terms 'Scripture' and 'Word of God.'"[109] However, if the evidence clearly warrants the conclusion that Scripture *is* the Word of God (and it does), then to question it, criticize it, dissect it, and destroy it may be considered an attack upon God. It is, after all, *His* Word. There isn't a man or woman alive who wouldn't respect and cherish the personal letters written to them by their loved ones. The fact that higher critics treat God's letters to us in the fashion they do underscores their rejection of God's love for them.

When it comes to issues of divine revelation and salvation, man—and especially critics, with Job, must remain silent because it is God who speaks. Like Moses, they must take the shoes off their feet for they stand on holy ground. With Isaiah they must confess "Woe to me...because I am a man of unclean lips (6:5)." We are, after all, speaking of the gracious revelation of an infinite God whose holiness is fearful. For sinners to stand in judgment on God's holy Word makes about as much sense as a dying patient standing before a world-class surgeon and criticizing his surgical competence. Although the surgeon has proven his expertise, the patient refuses to believe it. Even though his very life is at stake, he denies the surgeon the right to perform the surgery that would save him. How much more foolish is it for us, as sinners facing an eternal death, to sit in judgment upon the one who has so freely offered us the surgery of salvation? When higher critics attack Scripture, it is *not* only Scripture they attack. They attack the God who gave it to us and His Son—for He was the Word who became flesh: "In the beginning was the Word, and the Word was with God, and the Word was God.... The Word became flesh and made his dwelling among us" (John 1:1,14). Jesus was so clearly the personal revelation of God that He may be called the Word of God. To attack the Word of God is to attack God in a more direct manner than is usually realized.

As Walter Maier once warned, "It is not only an absolutely useless but also a manifestly sinful and extremely dangerous exercise for Christian pastors and people to take the gospels in hand and then to discard vital and substantial portions of the sacred text as though these were records of deliberate fabrications, mythological formulations, and misunderstanding on the part of the early Christian communities. Such a treatment of the evangelical material, involving the exaltation of (faulty) human reason over the divine revelation as it does, represents an unbelieving, rebellious despising of God's Word. It is a serious affront to the gracious Lord, who gave His truth to us, and is fraught with the gravest spiritual consequences."[110]

10. Are the benefits to the church worth the risk?

The major problem with higher criticism involves not just its cost to society, but also the cost to the church. In either case, the cost/benefit ratio is almost nil. In other words, what we have learned and benefited from higher criticism is virtually nothing compared to what it has negatively wrought in the church in terms of commitment to biblical inerrancy, authority, and study of the Word of God. If the history of higher criticism, from its inception to the present, reveals a revolt against God, then Christians should reject the methodology whose premises are so thoroughly opposed to the God of the Scriptures.

Let's look at the evangelical use of redaction criticism. Gerhard Maier says redaction criticism is a term that is applied to the most recent development in higher criticism and also a reaction of sorts against form criticism. He points out that redaction criticism accepts that the writers of the Gospels were biased theologians and not historians. "To develop their own respective theologies, they ascribed to Jesus words He never spoke and they credit Him with things He never did. These 'inventions' were necessary, according to this theory, in order to have a basis for the theology the writers *wanted* to develop."[111]

Sadly,

> the total approach of "redactional critical" studies published by evangelicals thus far tends to incorporate presuppositions of radical criticism which challenge the historical accuracy of parts of the gospel accounts."[115]

This is unacceptable for any Christian. (See notes 112-16.)

Is it possible for evangelicals to logically claim they believe in biblical inerrancy and simultaneously employ redaction criticism? No. Does their very method, with its faulty presuppositions, undermine a full allegiance to Scripture? Yes.

"Redaction Criticism: Is It Worth the Risk?" points out that many who use this method do so in order to have dialogue with their liberal or secular colleagues, hoping to promote the academic credibility of evangelicalism.

First, if we are going to be missionaries to the liberals, is there any evidence that our attempts will be successful? Dr. D.A. Carson comments, "I thought about that a great deal when I was at Cambridge as a doctoral student. I did a quick check on the non-evangelical doctoral supervisors who in the last 40–50 years had guided a significant number of evangelical students. I wanted to find out if any had been dramatically influenced by their students. I found only one who made a major theological change: R.V.G. Tasker. The rest of them—no."[117]

There is certainly little problem involved with someone well-grounded both academically and spiritually seeking to understand higher criticism in order to point out its problems or to let others understand that we know where they're coming from.[118] But it's another thing entirely to employ the methods on the biblical text or to risk his or her spiritual health. This may be at risk if he or she delves into areas not adequately prepared for.

Another area to evaluate for the cost/benefit ratio is the biblical text itself. Has 200 years of higher criticism given us any new information about the Bible? No! Vern Poythress illustrates this with the following important comment: "I recently [read] Marshall's commentary on Luke. A third of that commentary discusses redactional issues. For the most part, Marshall did a reasonable job with those questions. But when I asked myself, *What did I learn from his discussion of the sources?* the answer was, *Almost nothing*. I learned much more from what he had to say about the gospel itself. In my own exegetical work I found redaction criticism gives very little input in terms of the meaning of the final text."[119] What are we losing spiritually by spending hundreds of hours with critical methods dissecting the text when we could have spent that time reverently learning the text?

Another important point is that redaction criticism, like all forms of higher criticism, is unable to give us anything that could not be discovered by some other means. Dr. Carson points out, "If I were asked to identify something redaction criticism alone could point out [about the biblical text], my answer would be, precious little."[120 (cf.121)]

Robert Thomas, a New Testament professor at Talbot Theological Seminary, points out that the tendency among evangelicals is to not limit themselves to the "positive" aspects of redaction criticism but also to buy into other more problematic areas: "The specimens of evangelical criticism that have been forthcoming thus far have not limited themselves to [redaction aspects of] selectivity, arrangement, and minor modification. They have also included major modification and creativity. For example, Bob Gundry's commentary on Matthew, Howard Marshall's commentary on Luke, and Bill Lane's commentary on Mark follow a grammatical-*critical*-historical method of interpretation, allowing critical presuppositions to override the forthright historical meaning of the text. Gundry does this most often, Marshall not quite so often, and Lane only rarely. But they all do it."[122]

Gundry himself once wrote that form criticism "prejudices historical inquiry and is theologically and scientifically out of date, for it rests on the rationalistic concept of a closed universe and a rigid concept of natural law."[123] Gundry, of course, is specifically employing redaction criticism; however, this is based on form criticism and not that different in terms of consequences.

This raises the issue of the slippery slope or domino effect. Regardless of how little a given evangelical scholar engages in critical methodology, what is there to guarantee his "little" won't become a lot? Even with a little we may have problems: "When critical presuppositions so dominate, subjective judgments become the rule and the historicity of the text is open to all sorts of doubt, such as the question of how many of the eight beatitudes of Matthew 5 Jesus uttered. Did he give four, as Gundry contends, or was it only three, as Bob Guelich in his commentary on the Sermon on the Mount holds? It is a foregone conclusion with these two evangelicals that he could *not* have spoken all eight, as a natural understanding of Matthew would require. When the critical, subjective element intervenes, doubt about the historical accuracy of Matthew is inevitable."[124]

Can genuine redaction criticism be done at all without at least some degree of doubt emerging over the historical accuracy of the text? As Dr. Vern Poythress observes:

> Some of the really serious issues raised, in the Gundry affair in particular, get at the very essence of our view of Scripture. For example, are the Gospels history or are they semifictional? On the right wing of evangelicalism, people are saying, "If you can arbitrarily decide what genre a scriptural text is, then you can virtually destroy the authority of Scripture in practice. You can pretend to believe it all but say it doesn't mean what everyone has always thought. The Virgin Birth and the Resurrection—they're all great teaching devices whether they really happened or not. You can maintain that fiction teaches great principles even if historicity is absent." This is a statement of legitimate fear: if you open the doors with no control, you will destroy biblical authority.[125]

The comments of Kenneth Kantzer are also appropriate: "Many evangelicals are deeply concerned by the rise of this new discipline and fear and it will be used to destroy the evangelical view of Scripture. And the danger is real. In the hands [of] liberals it has done just that."[126]

But another issue is just as germane: There will always be *some* method of criticism. We can rest assured that when one critical methodology is found wanting, skeptics will devise another. It is their nature to do so. As Dr. Harold Hoehner points out, the heyday of source criticism lasted from the turn of the century to World War I; form criticism dominated to the end of the second world war; and redaction criticism has occupied center stage since. But it's only a matter of time before redaction criticism is replaced with something else.

The process will never stop, nor will the large amount of damage done by critical methods in comparison to the benefits of learning. This brings us to the third area of cost/benefit ratio: the theological consequences in the lives of Christians. The first issue involved the issue of "missionary" success (almost none); the second issue involved whether we gained any new important data about the biblical text (almost none); the third issue involves the impact on our doctrine of inerrancy (almost total).

We are convinced that the conclusions of Dr. John Warwick Montgomery are correct: "There is simply *no way* to employ critical techniques and 'yet carefully safeguard the full inerrancy of Scripture.'.... Inerrancy becomes a totally plastic concept at the mercy of the critical hermeneutic.... It renders it technically meaningless.... The evangelical committed to the inerrancy of Scripture must do just the reverse of what Osborne and Gundry do: he must allow the overall biblical concept of truth ... to give him his concept of inerrancy; that concept of inerrancy will create the hermeneutic limits for his handling of particular scriptural problems."[127]

Further, if the Gospel writers put words into Jesus' mouth, aren't *they* engaging in deception? And when we say that Jesus did things He didn't do, aren't *we* engaging in deception? Please read carefully what Dr. Montgomery writes:

> Take Osborne's example of the Great Commission. He declares that "It seems most likely that at some point the tradition or Matthew expanded an original monodic formula." Jesus, in other words, did not make a Trinitarian statement; the early church or Matthew expanded Jesus' monodic statement to become a Trinitarian statement; nevertheless, since God *is* a Trinity, the Holy Spirit was at work bringing about an inerrant result anyway! Now surely it ought to be obvious that the exegetical issue is not whether *Trinitarian* theology is inerrantly true, but whether the biblical writers can be trusted when they affirm that Jesus *said* something. Any meaningful doctrine of inerrancy requires that whether Jesus spoke in Aramaic, or Swahili, He in fact made reference to the Father, the Son, and the Holy Spirit on the occasion recorded in Matthew 28:19 [... baptizing them in the name of the Father and of the Son and of the Holy Spirit]. Otherwise, it would be obvious that the underlying question of what Jesus in fact said and did ends up totally severed from the question of the "inerrancy" of the edited text.... The Holy Spirit becomes a subjective justification for accepting a book that continually makes statements about what Jesus said and did that do not necessarily reflect accurately the details of the ministry that He in fact had. This is pure schwarmerei."[128]

Montgomery goes on to point out that when he majored in Greek and Latin classics at Cornell, he—

> discovered that the very techniques [of higher criticism] were weighed in the balance and found wanting in classical scholarship. My professors never tired of demonstrating the foolishness of 19th century attempts

"finding the true and original meaning" of classical texts through redaction and tradition criticism. With tremendous difficulty, classical scholarship pulled itself out of the "conjectural" morass of 19th century scholarship. Now classicists go back to the principles of harmonization set forth in Aristotle's *Poetics* to deal with discrepancies, stylistic variations, etc. The entire history of Western law works on the same basis of harmonization in the "construction of documentations." (wills, probate, executed deeds, etc.) It is simply appalling to me that people like Osborne and Gundry continue to work with conjectural methodology that no one today gives two whoops for outside of the Biblical field. C.S. Lewis was precisely correct from the standpoint of English literary scholarship when he argued that tradition and redaction criticism are irredeemable—and his position on the inerrancy of Scripture was considerably weaker than ETS [The Evangelical Theological Society] is supposed to maintain.[129]

Montgomery concludes: "By now, I should hope that it would be evident that Osborne, Gundry, and company do in fact 'falsify the Gospel accounts', for the 'inerrant' resultant text can and does often present a *false* picture of what Jesus actually said and did. Whether one attaches the word 'inerrant' to the result is really of little consequence."[130]

Finally, consider the highly relevant comments of the Cambridge and Oxford scholar C.S. Lewis concerning higher criticism applied to his own works:

> I have watched with some care similar imaginary histories both of my own books and of books of friends whose real history I knew. Reviewers, both friendly and hostile, will dash you off such histories with great confidence; will tell you what public events had directed the author's mind to this or that, what other authors had influenced him, what his over-all intention was, what sort of audience he principally addressed, why—and when—he did everything.
>
> Now I must first record my impression; then, distinct from it, what I can say with certainty. My impression is that in the whole of my experience not one of these guesses has on any one point been right; that the method shows a record of 100 percent failure. You would expect that by mere chance they would hit as often as they miss. But it is my impression that they do no such thing. I can't remember a single hit. But as I have not kept a careful record my mere impression may be mistaken.

> What I think I can say with certainty is that they are usually wrong.
>
> And yet they would often sound—if you didn't know the truth—extremely convincing.... Now this surely ought to give us pause. The reconstruction of the history of a text, when the text is ancient, sounds very convincing. But one is after all sailing by dead reckoning; the results cannot be checked by fact. In order to decide how reliable the method is at work and we have facts to check it by? Well, that is what I have done. And we find, that when this check is available, the results are either always, or else nearly always, wrong. The "assured results of modern scholarship," as to the way in which an old book was written, are "assured," we may conclude, only because the men who knew the facts are dead and can't blow the gaff....
>
> The superiority in judgement and diligence which you are going to attribute to the biblical critics will have to be almost superhuman if it is to offset the fact that they are everywhere faced with customs, language, race-characteristics, class-characteristics, a religious background, habits of composition, and basic assumption, which no scholarship will ever enable any man now alive to know as surely and intimately and instinctively as the reviewer can know mine. And for the very same reason, remember, the Biblical critics, whatever reconstructions they devise, can never be crudely proved wrong. St. Mark is dead. When they meet St. Peter there will be more pressing matters to discuss.[131]

In conclusion, the extremely small amount of value, if any, of higher criticism seems completely eclipsed by the tremendous damage it does. *This* is what raises the question of evangelical involvement in such methods.

Perhaps the only truly valid consequence of higher criticism can be seen by default—in its utter failure to demonstrate the validity of its assumptions and the truth of its conclusions; by forfeiture it has strengthened the conservative view of Scripture.

Recommended Reading

Donald Guthrie in his *New Testament Introduction* (Inter-Varsity Press), according to Cal Beisner, "Thoroughly decimates liberal critical views of NT books." R.K. Harrison does the same for the Old Testament in his *Introduction to Old Testament*.

A.F. Johnson. "The Historical-Critical Method: Egyptian Gold or Pagan Precipice?", *Journal of the Evangelical Theological Society*, vol. 26, no. 1, 1983, pp. 3-15.

John Warwick Montgomery. "Why Has God Incarnate Suddenly Become Mythical?" *Perspectives on Evangelical Theology*, Kenneth Kantzer and S.N. Gundry, eds. Grand Rapids: Baker, 1979, pp. 57-65. A strong criticism of modern critical methods.

NOTES

1. Cited in *Atlantic Monthly,* Dec. 1996.

2. "The Search for Jesus" *(Time),* "Rethinking the Resurrection" *(Newsweek);* "In Search of Jesus" *(U.S. News and World Report).*

3. George Barna, *What Americans Believe* (Ventura, CA: Regal Books, 1991), from Adjith Fernando, *The Supremacy of Christ* (Wheaton, IL: Crossway Books, 1995) p. 20, in *Christian Research Journal,* Winter 1995, p. 50; *Newsweek,* April 8, 1996, p. 62.

4. See our *Behind the Mask of Mormonism* and *The Facts on Islam* (Harvest House Publishers).

5. Other books include: Marcus Borg, *Meeting Jesus Again for the First Time;* Geza Vermes, *Jesus the Jew;* Barbara Thiering, *Jesus the Man: A New Interpretation of the Dead Sea Scrolls;* A.N. Wilson, *Jesus: A Life;* John Shelby Spong, *Born of a Woman: A Bishop Rethinks the Birth of Jesus;* Ian Wilson, *Jesus: The Evidence;* John Allegro, *The Sacred Mushroom and the Cross;* David Spangler, *Reflections on the Christ;* S.G.S. Brandon, *Jesus and the Zealots;* and Morton Smith, *The Secret Gospel* and *Jesus the Magician.*

6. Jeffrey L. Sheler, "In Search of Jesus," *U.S. News and World Report,* April 8, 1996, pp. 47-48.

7. David van Biema, "The Gospel Truth(?)" *Time,* April 8, 1996, p. 54.

8. Ibid., p. 57.

9. Unfortunately, Johnson's own book, *The Real Jesus,* retreats into subjectivism as well, probably due to his Catholic background and its own infection with higher criticism. Here is an illustration of Johnson's problematic methodology: "Christianity has never been able to 'prove' its claims except by appeal to the experiences and convictions of those already convinced. The only real validation for the claim that Jesus is what the creed claims him to be, light from light, true God from true God, is to be found in the quality of life demonstrated by those who make this confession." But what about the historic fact of the resurrection (Romans 1:4) or fulfilled messianic prophecy (Luke 24:44). These prove objectively that Jesus is God. In the words of biblical scholar N.T. Wright, Johnson's approach here is poppycock. "He kicks the ball back into his own net by mistake" (cited in van Biema, "Gospel Truth"). In other words, Johnson falls into a similar quagmire of subjectivism that the Jesus Seminar has been reveling in all along. Thus, it is just as much nonsense to say that the only thing that proves Christianity true is subjective experience and lifestyle as it is to say that little or nothing in the Gospels is historically credible. If we argue that the only proof of Christianity is found subjectively, then *it makes no difference* whether or not the Gospels are historically reliable. If what Johnson says is correct, that "the faith of most Christians is sustained principally by the witness of the Holy Spirit in their daily lives," then how can we know what the Holy Spirit witnesses *to* if we can't even know *who* Jesus is or that the New Testament records are *accurate*? "Christianity," says Johnson, "is an organic, evolving religion based, above all, on personal leaps and tests of faith." Johnson, who received his Ph.D. at the liberal Yale University in 1976, says his own most sacred religious beliefs are confirmed in experience, not in texts." (Sheler, "In Search," p. 53). Wright is correct. This is poppycock. Cited in van Biema, "Gospel Truth," p. 58.

10. John Dart, "Skepticism of Many New Testament Scholars Clashes with Laymen's Faith and Traditional Beliefs on Jesus," *Los Angeles Times,* April 27, 1985, part II, p. 8.

11. Ibid.

12. Richard N. Ostling, "Who Was Jesus?" *Time,* Aug. 15, 1988, p. 42.

13. Robert W. Funk, Roy W. Hoover, and the Jesus Seminar, *The Five Gospels: The Search for the Authentic Words of Jesus* (New York: MacMillan, 1993), p. 34.

14. Ibid., p. 36.

15. In spite of its bias against women (Gos. Thom, p. 114); see Funk, Hoover, the Jesus Seminar, *Five Gospels*, p. 15; and Gregory A. Boyd, *Cynic, Sage or Son of God?* (Wheaton, IL: Bridge Point, 1995), pp. 79, 132-35, 150.

16. Funk, Hoover, the Jesus Seminar, *Five Gospels*, p. 5.

17. Gregory A. Boyd, *Cynic, Sage or Son of God?* (Wheaton, IL: Bridge Point, 1995), pp. 61, 127.

18. See, for example, Allan A. MacRae, "The Canon of Scripture: Can We Be Sure Which Books Are Inspired by God?" in John Warwick Montgomery, ed. *Evidence for Faith: Deciding the God Question* (Dallas: Probe Books, 1991), pp. 215-30.

19. Boyd, *Cynic*, pp. 150, 151.

20. A & E TV channel, "Mysteries of the Bible: Heaven and Hell," Oct. 3, 1996.

21. "Who Was Jesus? Reflections on the Jesus Seminar," *Theological Students Fellowship Bulletin*, Feb. 1994, p. 3.

22. Funk, Hoover, and Jesus Seminar, *Five Gospels*, p. 34.

23. Adjith Fernando, *The Supremacy of Christ*, (Wheaton, IL: Crossway Books, 1995), p. 19.

24. Funk, Hoover and the Jesus Seminar, *Five Gospels*, p. 34.

25. Ibid., pp. 4, 5, 7, 24, emphasis added.

26. Ibid., pp. xviii, 34-35.

27. Kenneth L. Woodward, "Rethinking the Resurrection," *Newsweek*, April 8, 1996, p. 70.

28. From Craig L. Blomberg, *The Historical Reliability of the Gospels* (Downer's Grove, IL: InterVarsity Press, 1987), p. xii.

29. Boyd, *Cynic*, p. 11.

30. Funk, Hoover, the Jesus Seminar, *Five Gospels*, pp. 533-37.

31. James Parker, III, "Jesus' Scholarship," *Religious and Theological Studies Fellowship Bulletin*, Feb. 1994, p. 2.

32. Sheler, "In Search of Jesus," p. 48, emphasis added.

33. Ibid., p. 49; R.W. Funk, "The Issue of Jesus," *Foundations and Facets Forum*, vol. 1, no. 1 (1985), p. 12, cited in Boyd, *Cynic*, p. 60.

34. Cited in Charlotte Allen, "The Search for a No Frills Jesus," *The Atlantic Monthly*, Dec. 1996, p. 67.

35. In Boyd, *Cynic*, p. 61.

36. Michael J. Wilkins and J.P. Moreland, *Jesus Under Fire: Modern Scholarship Reinvents the Historical Jesus* (Grand Rapids, MI: Zondervan, 1995), p. 186, citing John P. Meier, "The Testimonium: Evidence for Jesus Outside the Bible," *Bible Review* 7 (June 1991), p. 22.

37. Adapted from Boyd, *Cynic*, p. 10.

38. It's really quite amazing that liberal scholars are still debating the same old issues kept alive *only* by their own philosophical and theological biases. What the liberal theologians are saying today would in an earlier era have been condemned as heresy. In effect, by claiming to be Christian and to defend Christianity, all the while deliberately seeking to undermine it, the liberal theologians are almost forcing a return to the heresy trials of the past. This was recently illustrated with the charges brought against Episcopal Bishop John Spong and his advocacy of homosexual ordination and other radical or heretical teachings. Spong claims to be a committed Christian: "Jesus lives. I have seen the Lord. By that faith and with that conviction I live my life and proclaim my gospel" (*Resurrection: Myth or Reality: A Bishop's Search for the Origins of Christianity* [San Francisco: Harper, 1994], p. 282, cf., XI, XII, 292). Yet he denies and opposes the most basic Christian teachings:

a. Jesus: "The simplistic suggestion that Jesus is God is nowhere made in the Bible story. Nowhere!" (*This Hebrew Lord*, p. 143).

I have dismissed many of the later-written [i.e., New Testament] details of Easter as legends . . . " (*Resurrection*, p. 289).

b. The Bible: "That word [the true Word of God] is not to be identified with the words of Scripture but is found in, with, through, and beyond these words" (*Living in Sin*, p. 156).

"[The New Testament text is] quite untrustworthy if what we [are] seeking [is] objective facts and consistent detail" (*Resurrection: Myth or Reality*, p. 235).

"This is not an attack on the integrity of the Bible. . . . It is rather an attack on a literalistic and magical view of Holy Scripture that I believe imprisons the real truth of the Bible. Unless we succeed in supplanting fundamentalistic interpretations of the Bible, the Bible itself will be rendered impotent and valueless in a very short period of time" (*Living in Sin*, p. 93).

c. Sin: "Sin is ontological, not moral" (*This Hebrew Lord*, p. 68).

d. Salvation: "To bring that love that creates wholeness is to be the savior of humankind" (*This Hebrew Lord*, p. 173).

e. Atonement: "Jesus could not be . . . the 'substitute savior' that so many theories of the atonement seem to suggest. . . . A God who would crucify Jesus to satisfy an offended sense of justice is no God for our generation. A 'substitute savior' will not translate in our day, if indeed it ever really did" (*This Hebrew Lord,* p. 172).

f. Heaven and Hell: "I have no interest in the reward/punishment aspect of the afterlife;" "Every writer in the New Testament seems to have believed something different about the afterlife. There is no hell, for example, in Paul's writings" (*Resurrection*, p. 283).

"Hell is the absence of meaning, the destruction of life, the loneliness of isolation. . . . [But] Jesus' resurrection reveals my ultimate destiny and yours. It is nothing less than the fullness of life which flows into eternity" (*The Easter Moment*, pp. 222-23).

"[God will bring] all people into unity with God, with each other, and with themselves (Isaiah 53:10ff.)" (*This Hebrew Lord*, p. 106).

g. The Ten Commandments: "The [ten] commandments are . . . blunt, dogmatic, and straightforward, leaving little room for a post-Freudian emphasis on motivation" (*Beyond Moralism*, p. 20).

h. The Resurrection of Christ: "The details in the resurrection narratives of the Bible clearly do not refer to physical categories. . . . These are clearly non-*physical* symbols" (*The Easter Moment*, pp. 112-13). "If the resurrection of Christ cannot be believed except by assenting to fantastic descriptions included in the Gospels, then Christianity is doomed. For that view of the resurrection is not believable" (*Resurrection: Myth or Reality?* p. 238).

i. The Trinity: "The patriarchal worldview has been identified with the patriarchal God, as defined by the patriarchal hierarchy of the patriarchal church. . . . The categories of Christian theology (God as Father, Son and Holy Ghost) make this obvious" (*Living in Sin*, p. 220).

"So we must clear out the rubbish of a religious point of view that is not more bury the God who is dead, weep no more for that God" (*This Hebrew Lord*, p. 59).

"And who is God? God is not a figure in the sky who thinks and acts, who feels and directs. God is the source of life. God is seen wherever life is lived, and God is not alien or separated from that life. . . . God is the ground of being.... And God is not alien or separated from that being" (*This Hebrew Lord*, p. 143).

j. Morality: "For the church not to recognize that its traditional moral codes rise out of, enforce, and interpret a system of male oppression of women is irresponsible.... I, for one, am no longer willing to acknowledge the claim that morality has been frozen in an era that primarily served the dominant male. Nor do I share a sense of regret that this moral understanding is passing away" (*Living in Sin*, p. 66).

"The church must abandon its irrelevant ethical judgments that arise from realities that no longer exist" (*Living in Sin*, p. 217).

"As one voice in the church, I am not prepared to condemn nonconventional sexual relationships that are issuing in enhanced life" (*Living in Sin*, p. 175).

k. God: "God is the life force ... the Being at the depths of our being"; "I no longer look for God or for ultimate meaning in some distant place beyond this world" (*Resurrection*, pp. 289-90).

39. The information cited is based on Dennis Ingolfsland (Brian College), "Burton Mack's Revision of Christian History," a March 1996 scholarly critique of *Who Wrote the New Testament: The Making of the Christian Myth* (San Francisco: Harper, 1995), citing p. 306.

40. Ibid., citing p. 206.

41. Ibid., citing p. 307, emphasis added.

42. Ibid., citing p. 145.

43. Dennis Ingolfsland (Brian College), "Burton Mack's Revision of Christian History," March 1996, pp. 19-20.

44. John Warwick Montgomery, *Faith Founded on Fact: Essays in Evidential Apologetics* (Nashville: Thomas Nelson, 1978), pp. 168-69.

45. Walter A. Maier, *Form Criticism Reexamined* (St. Louis: Concordia Publishing House, 1973), pp. 32-33.

46. William Lane Craig, *The Son Rises* (Chicago: Moody Press, 1981), pp. 135-36.

47. Michael J. Wilkins and J.P. Moreland, "Introduction: The Furor Surrounding Jesus," *Jesus Under Fire*, pp. 6, 11.

48. Cited in Montgomery, *Faith Founded on Fact*, p. 87.

49. Craig L. Blomberg, "Where Do We Start Studying Jesus?" in Wilkins and Moreland, *Jesus Under Fire*, p. 19.

50. Craig L. Blomberg, "The Seventy-Four 'Scholars': Who Does the Jesus Seminar Really Speak For?" *Christian Research Journal*, Fall 1994, p. 37.

51. Craig L. Blomberg, "Where Do We Start," pp. 20, 21.

52. William Lane Craig, "Did Jesus Rise from the Dead?" in Wilkins and Moreland, *Jesus Under Fire*, p. 142.

53. John Dominic Crossan, *The Historical Jesus: The Life of a Mediterranean Jewish Peasant* (San Francisco: Harper, 1992), p. 423.

54. Ibid., p. xxvii.

55. Wilkins and Moreland, *Jesus Under Fire*, pp. 2, 4, 8-9.

56. Funk, Hoover, the Jesus Seminar, *Five Gospels*, p. 2.

57. Wilkins and Moreland, *Jesus Under Fire*, p. 10.

58. Craig, "Did Jesus Rise," pp. 144-46.

59. Funk, Hoover, the Jesus Seminar, *Five Gospels*, pp. 16-33.

60. Ibid., p. 16.

61. Ibid., p. 19.

62. Ibid., p. 21.

63. Ibid., p. 23.

64. Craig, "Did Jesus Rise," p. 162.

65. Blomberg, *Historical Reliability*, pp. 246-48, 253, 254.

66. E.g., John Warwick Montgomery, "The Jury Returns: A Juridical Defense of Christianity," in his *Evidence for Faith: Deciding the God Question* (Dallas: Probe Books, 1991), pp. 319-42.

67. Darrell L. Bock, "The Words of Jesus in the Gospels: Live, Jive, or Memorex?" in Wilkins and Moreland, *Jesus Under Fire*, pp. 92-93.

68. Funk, Hoover, the Jesus Seminar, *Five Gospels*, p. 5. The last statement was colored red for emphasis; we italicized it.

69. Ibid., p. 5.

70. Ibid., pp. 5, 35.

71. Ibid., p. 16.

72. Ibid., p. 543.

73. Woodward, "Rethinking the Resurrection," pp. 62-63.

74. Robert J. Hutchinson, "The Jesus Seminar Unmasked," *Christianity Today*, April 29, 1996, pp. 28-29.

75. Gary R. Habermas, "Did Jesus Perform Miracles?" in Wilkins and Moreland, *Jesus Under Fire*, p.128.

76. In Blomberg, "Seventy-Four 'Scholars,'" p. 29.

77. See the article by Allen in the *Atlantic Monthly*, December 1996, p. 56.

78. John Wenham, *Redating Matthew, Mark and Luke* (Downer's Grove, IL: InterVarsity Press, 1992), p. 3.

79. Ibid., p. 1.

80. Wenham, *Redating Matthew, Mark and Luke*, p. 42.

81. Boyd, *Cynic*, p. 142.

82. Ibid.

83. Hutchinson, "Jesus Seminar Unmasked," p. 28.

84. Blomberg, "Seventy-Four 'Scholars,'" p. 37.

85. Woodward, "Rethinking the Resurrection," p. 70.

86. See Gary Habermas, *The Historical Jesus: Ancient Evidence for the Life of Christ* (Joplin, MO: College Press Publishing Co., 1996).

87. Interview, *Saturday Evening Post*, Oct. 26, 1929, cited in Arthur W. Kac, *The Messiahship of Jesus: What Jesus and Jewish Christians Say* (Chicago: Moody, 1980), p. 40.

88. F.F. Bruce, foreword in Blomberg, *Historical Reliability*, p. ix.

89. The John Ankerberg Show transcript, "Jesus Christ: Was He a Liar, a Lunatic, a Legend or God?" (Chattanooga, TN: The John Ankerberg Show, 1988), pp. 7-8.

90. Boyd, *Cynic*, p. 163.

91. Scott McKnight, "Who Is Jesus? An Introduction to Jesus Studies," in Wilkins and Moreland, *Jesus Under Fire*, pp. 67-68.

92. Blomberg, "Where Do We Start," p. 44.

93. Craig, "Did Jesus Rise," p. 168.

94. Van Biema, "The Gospel Truth(?) p. 59.

95. Those who desire a more detailed refutation should consult Wilkins and Moreland, *Jesus Under Fire*; Boyd, *Cynic*; and N.T. Wright (who, until recently, taught New Testament at Oxford University), *Jesus and the Victory of God*, a 600-p. scholarly text which, among other things, demonstrates that

Christ's bodily resurrection has a sound historical basis. (Wright has also written a 40-p. critique of the Jesus Seminar, see N.T. Wright, "The New Unimproved Jesus," *Christianity Today*, Sep. 13, 1993.)

96. Walter A. Elwell, ed., *Evangelical Dictionary of Theology* (Grand Rapids: Baker Book House, 1994), p. 512.

97. Gordon Fee and Douglas Stuart's *How to Read the Bible for All Its Worth* and Mortimer Adler's *How to Read a Book* offer excellent illustrations.

98. W. Maier, *Form Criticism Reexamined*, p. 9.

99. The above summary was excerpted from W. Maier, *Form Criticism Reexamined*, pp. 7-10.

100. Ibid., p. 38.

101. In Boyd, *Cynic*, pp. 20-22; see chapters 5–11 for a critique of modern JS applications.

102. In Gerhard Maier, *The End of the Historical-Critical Method* (St. Louis: Concordia, 1974), p. 8.

103. Ibid., Foreword, p. 8.

104. Ostling, "Who Was Jesus?" p. 42.

105. G. Maier, *End of the Historical-Critical Method*, pp. 8-9.

106. Ibid., p. 11.

107. Ibid., p. 12.

108. Ibid., p. 10.

109. Ibid., p. 15.

110. W. A. Maier, *Form Criticism Reexamined*, p. 44.

111. G. Maier, *End of the Historical-Critical Method*, p. 108, emphasis added.

112. Ibid., p. 7.

113. Ibid.

114. Ibid., p. 8.

115. Ibid.

116. Ibid., p. 10.

117. "Redaction Criticism: Is It Worth the Risk?" Christianity Today Institute, *Christianity Today*, October 18, 1985, p. 7-I.

118. Ibid.

119. Ibid.

120. Ibid.

121. Ibid.

122. Ibid., p. 8-I.

123. Ibid., p. 8-I.

124. Ibid., emphasis added.

125. Ibid., p. 10-I.

126. Kenneth S. Kantzer, "Redaction Criticism: Handle with Care," in Ibid., p. 11-I.

127. John Warwick Montgomery, "Communication to Kenneth Kantzer in RE: Evangelical Use of Redaction Criticism," Xerox copy of undated paper.

128. Ibid.

129. Ibid.

130. Ibid., emphasis added.

131. C.S. Lewis, *Christian Reflections* (Grand Rapids, MI: Eerdmans), pp. 159-61.